HAL•LEONARD

pro vocal®
BETTER THAN KARAOKE!

SING 8 THEATRE FAVOURITES WITH A PROFESSIONAL BAND

R MALE SINGERS

SING ALONG
SHOWTUNES

SONGBOOK & SOUND-A-LIKE CD WITH UNIQUE PITCH-CHANGER™

R MALE SINGERS

SING 8 THEATRE FAVOURITES WITH A PROFESSIONAL BAND

SING ALONG
SHOWTUNES

SONGBOOK & SOUND-A-LIKE CD WITH UNIQUE PITCH-CHANGER™

HAL LEONARD EUROPE
Distributed by Music Sales

Exclusive Distributors:
Music Sales Limited
14-15 Berners Street, London W1T 3LJ, UK.

Order No. HLE90003804
ISBN 978-1-84938-005-8
This book © Copyright 2009 Hal Leonard Europe

Printed in the USA

Your Guarantee of Quality
As publishers, we strive to produce every book to the highest
commercial standards. The book has been carefully designed
to minimise awkward page turns and to make playing from it a
real pleasure. Throughout, the printing and binding have been
planned to ensure a sturdy, attractive publication which should
give years of enjoyment. If your copy fails to meet our high
standards, please inform us and we will gladly replace it.

www.musicsales.com

CONTENTS

PAGE	TITLE	DEMO TRACK	SING-ALONG TRACK
6	**ALL I ASK OF YOU** THE PHANTOM OF THE OPERA	1	9
10	**BRING HIM HOME** LES MISÉRABLES	2	10
18	**DON'T GET AROUND MUCH ANYMORE** SOPHISTICATED LADY	3	11
22	**GEORGIA ON MY MIND** RAY	4	12
13	**THE LADY IS A TRAMP** BABES IN ARMS	5	13
24	**THE SURREY WITH THE FRINGE ON TOP** OKLAHOMA!	6	14
28	**TRADITION** FIDDLER ON THE ROOF	7	15
37	**YOUNG AT HEART** YOUNG AT HEART	8	16

All I Ask Of You

from THE PHANTOM OF THE OPERA

Music by Andrew Lloyd Webber
Lyrics by Charles Hart
Additional Lyrics by Richard Stilgoe

1. No more talk of dark-ness, for-get these wide-eyed fears. I'm

here, noth-ing can harm you, my words will warm and calm you.

Let me be your free-dom, let day-light dry your tears. I'm

here, with you, be-side you, to guard you and to guide you.

Say you love me ev-'ry wak-ing mo-ment. Turn my head with talk of

sum - mer - time.   Say   you   need   me   with   you   now   and   al - ways.

Prom - ise me   that   all   you   say   is   true,   That's   all   I   ask   of

Verse

Female:

you.

Male:

2. Let   me   be   your shel - ter,   let   me   be   your light.   You're

Male:

safe,   no   one   will find   you,   your   fears   are   far   be - hind   you.

Female:

All   I   want   is   free - dom,   a   world   with   no   more night,   and

Female:

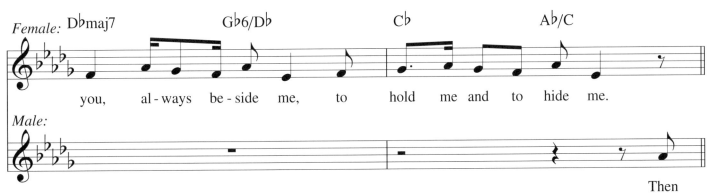

you,   al - ways be - side   me,   to   hold   me and   to   hide   me.

Male:

Then

7

Chorus

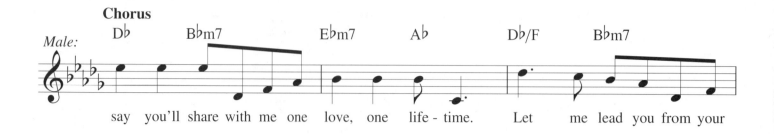

Male: say you'll share with me one love, one life - time. Let me lead you from your

sol - i - tude. Say you need me with you here, be - side you.

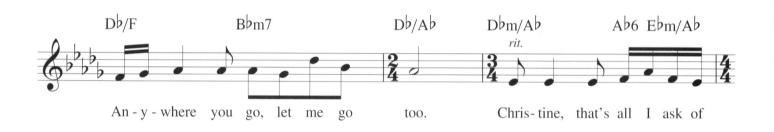

An - y - where you go, let me go too. Chris - tine, that's all I ask of

A tempo

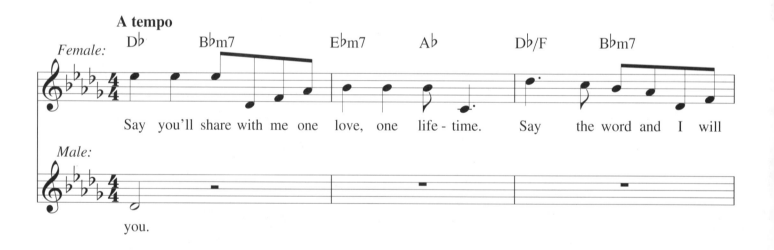

Female: Say you'll share with me one love, one life - time. Say the word and I will

Male: you.

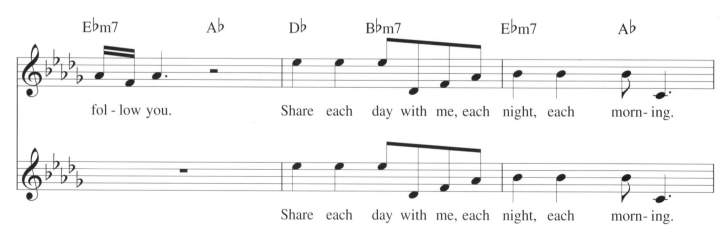

fol - low you. Share each day with me, each night, each morn - ing.

Share each day with me, each night, each morn - ing.

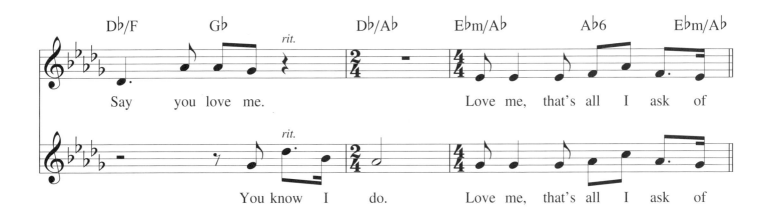

Say   you love me.   Love me, that's all I ask of

You know I do.   Love me, that's all I ask of

Outro
A tempo

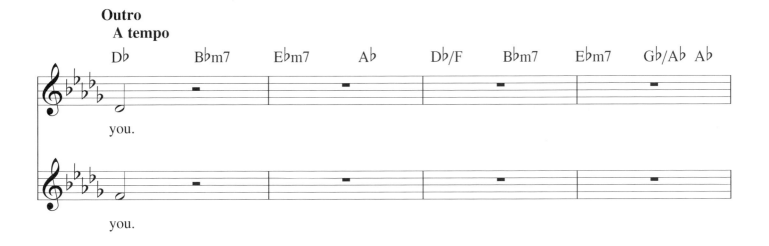

you.

you.

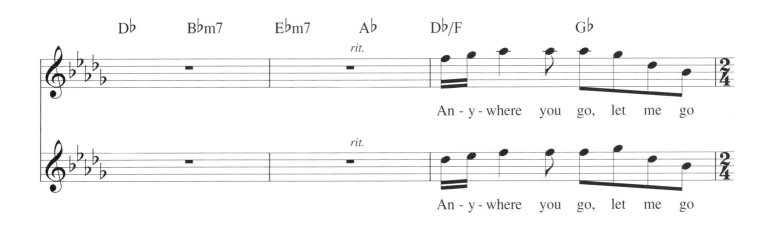

An - y - where you go, let me go

An - y - where you go, let me go

too.   Love me, that's all I ask of you.

too.   Love me, that's all I ask of you.

Bring Him Home

from LES MISÉRABLES

Music by Claude-Michel Schönberg
Lyrics by Alain Boublil and Herbert Kretzmer

God on

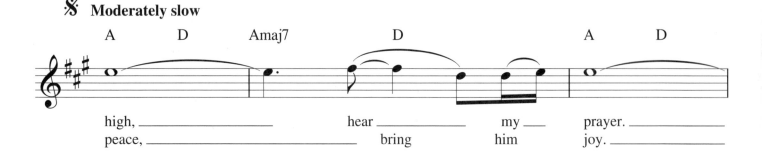

high, _____ hear ____ my ____ prayer. _____
peace, _____ bring him ____ joy. _____

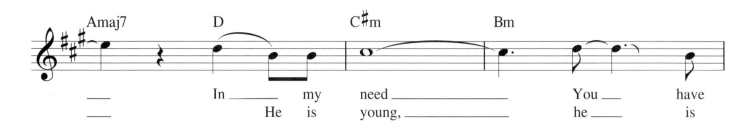

___ In ____ my need _____ You ____ have
___ He is young, _____ he ____ is

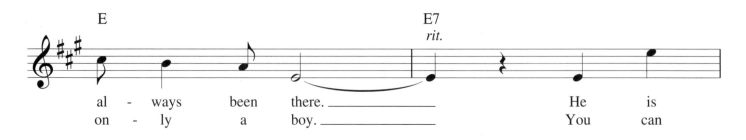

al - ways been there. _____ He is
on - ly a boy. _____ You can

A tempo

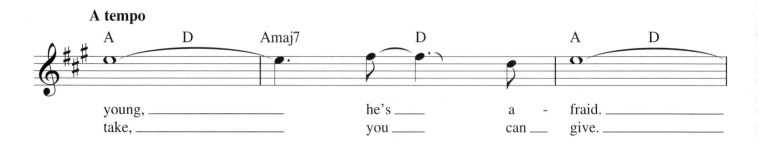

young, _____ he's ____ a - fraid. _____
take, _____ you ____ can ____ give. _____

Music and Lyrics Copyright © 1986 by Alain Boublil Music Ltd. (ASCAP)
Mechanical and Publication Rights for the U.S.A. Administered by Alain Boublil Music Ltd. (ASCAP)
c/o Stephen Tenenbaum & Co., Inc., 1775 Broadway, Suite 708, New York, NY 10019,
Tel. (212) 246-7204, Fax (212) 246-7217
International Copyright Secured. All Rights Reserved. This music is copyright. Photocopying is illegal.
All Performance Rights Restricted.

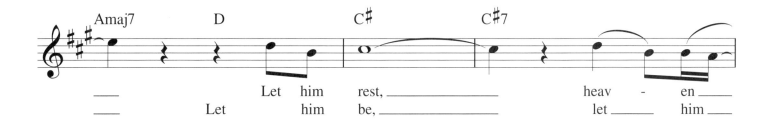

Let him rest, _____ heav - en _____
Let him be, _____ let him _____

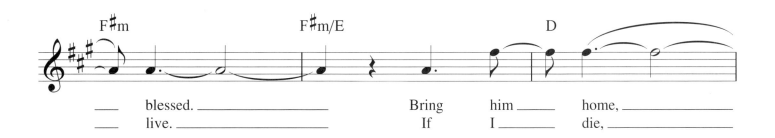

___ blessed. _____ Bring him _____ home, _____
___ live. _____ If I _____ die, _____

To Coda ⊕

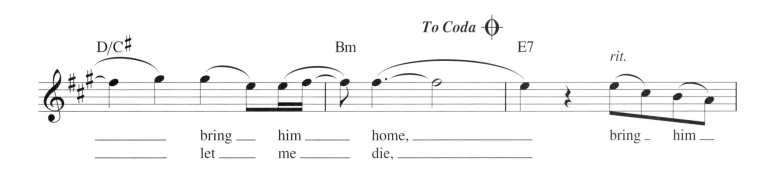

_____ bring _____ him _____ home, _____ bring _ him _____
_____ let _____ me _____ die, _____

A tempo

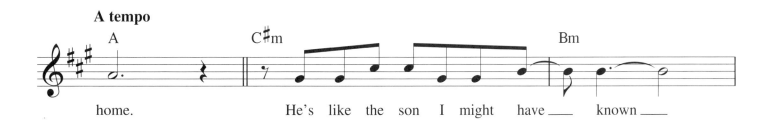

home. He's like the son I might have _____ known _____

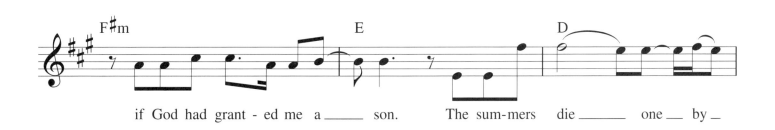

if God had grant - ed me a _____ son. The sum-mers die _____ one _ by _

one. How soon _ they ____ fly ____ on and ____ on. And I am

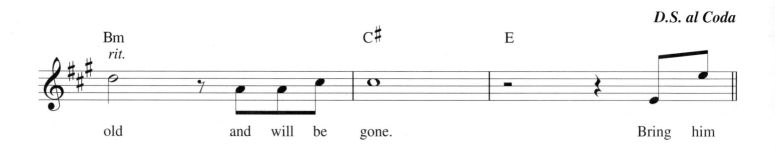

D.S. al Coda

old and will be gone. Bring him

Coda

A tempo

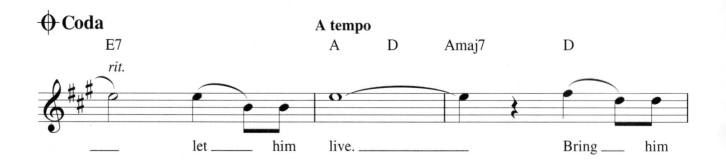

____ let ____ him live. _____ Bring ____ him

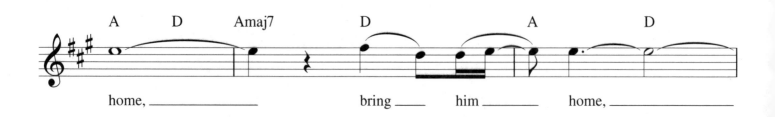

home, _____ bring ____ him _____ home, _____

A tempo

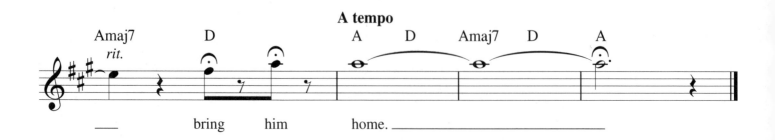

____ bring him home. _____

The Lady Is A Tramp

from BABES IN ARMS
Words by Lorenz Hart
Music by Richard Rodgers

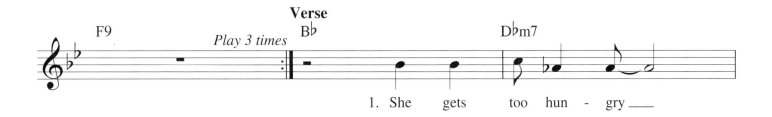

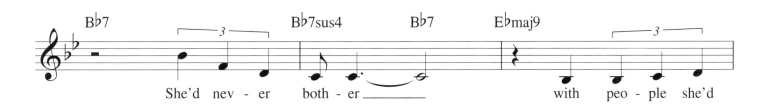

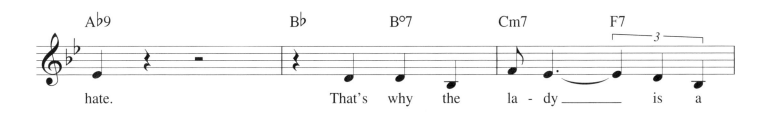

She's broke, and it's oke. 3. Hates Cal - i - for -

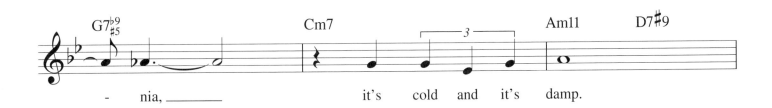

- nia, _____ it's cold and it's damp.

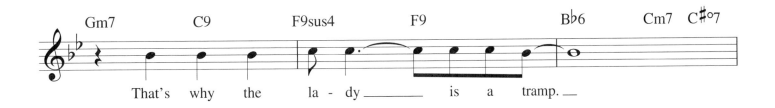

That's why the la - dy _____ is a tramp. _

4. She ___ gets too ___ hun - gry ___

to wait for din - ner at eight. She loves the thea -

- tre, _____ but nev - er comes late.

She'd nev - er both - er with peo - ple she'd hate. _

That's why the la-dy _____ is a tramp. _

5. She'll ___ have no ___

___ crap games _ with sharp-ies or frauds.

Won't go to Har - lem in ___ Lin-colns or Fords. _

___ She won't _ dish the dirt with

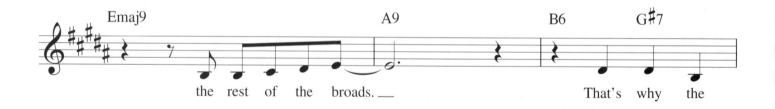

the rest of the broads. ___ That's why the

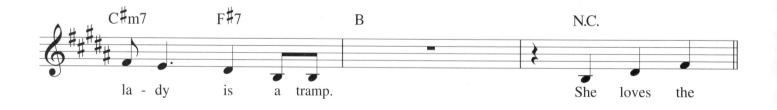

la - dy is a tramp. She loves the

Bridge

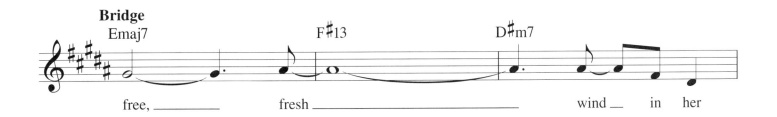

free, _____ fresh _____ wind _ in her

hair, life _____ with - out care.

She's broke, and it's oke.

Outro-Verse

Hates Cal - i - for - nia, _____ it's so cold and so

damp. That's why the la - dy, _____

that's why the la - dy, _____ that's why the la -

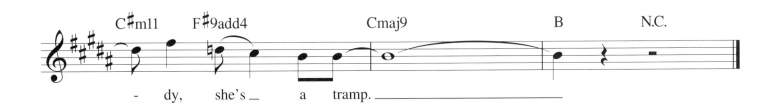

- dy, she's _ a tramp. _____

Don't Get Around Much Anymore

from SOPHISTICATED LADY

Words and Music by Duke Ellington and Bob Russell

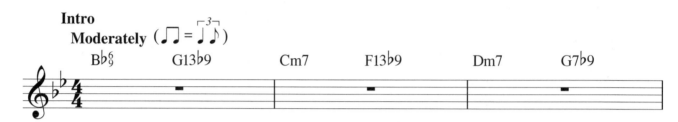

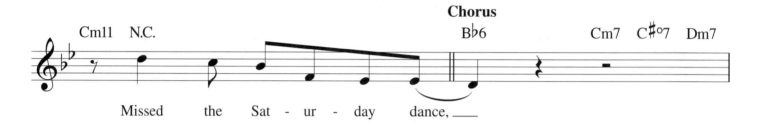

Missed the Sat - ur - day dance, ___

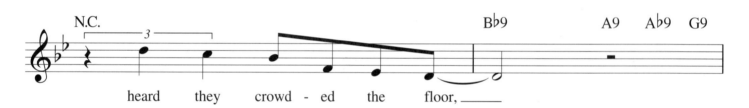

heard they crowd - ed the floor, ___

could - n't bear it with - out _____ you, ___

don't get a - round ___ much ___ an - y - more.

Thought I'd vis - it the club,

Well, ___ dar - ling, I guess ___ that my ___ mind's ___ more at

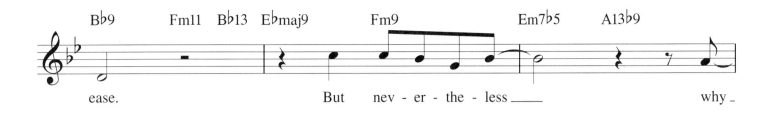

ease. But nev - er - the - less _____ why _

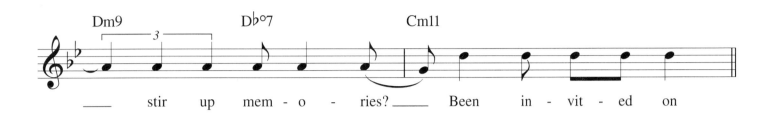

_____ stir up mem - o - ries? _____ Been in - vit - ed on

Outro-Chorus

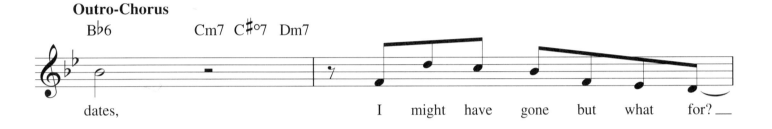

dates, I might have gone but what for? __

_____ Aw - f'lly dif - f'rent with - out _____

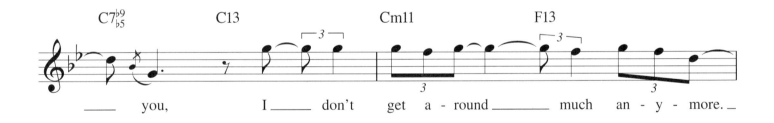

_____ you, I _____ don't get a - round _____ much an - y - more. _____

_____ No, ba - by, don't get a - round _

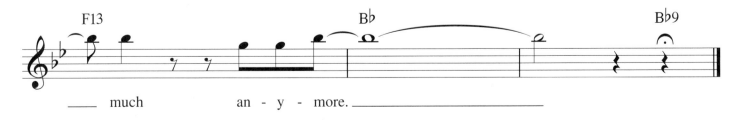

_____ much an - y - more. _____

Georgia On My Mind

from RAY

Words by Stuart Gorrell
Music by Hoagy Carmichael

The Surrey With The Fringe On Top

from OKLAHOMA!

Lyrics by Oscar Hammerstein II
Music by Richard Rodgers

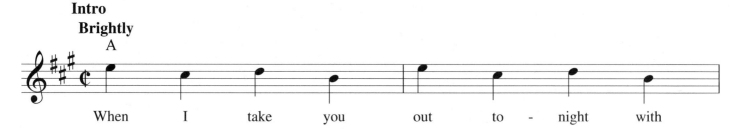

When I take you out to - night with

me, _____ hon - ey, here's the way it's gon - na

be. _____ You will set be - hind a team of

snow white hors - es, in the slick - est gig you've ev - er

Verse
Relaxed 2

seen. _____ Chicks and ducks and geese bet - ter scur - ry,

when I take you out in the sur - rey, when I take you

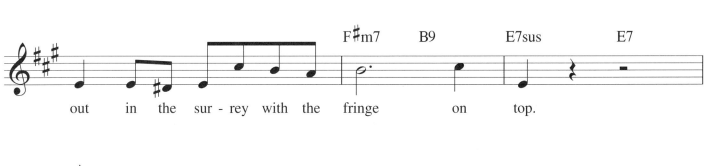

out in the sur - rey with the fringe on top.

Watch that fringe and see how it flut - ters, when I drive them

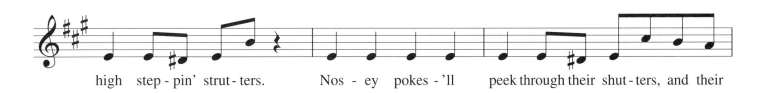

high step - pin' strut - ters. Nos - ey pokes - 'll peek through their shut - ters, and their

Bridge

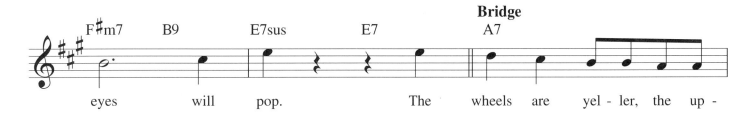

eyes will pop. The wheels are yel - ler, the up -

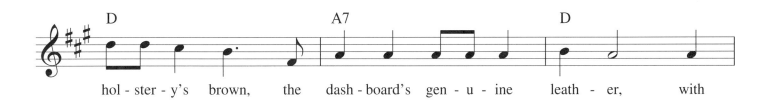

hol - ster - y's brown, the dash - board's gen - u - ine leath - er, with

i - sin - glass cur - tains you can roll right down, in

Verse

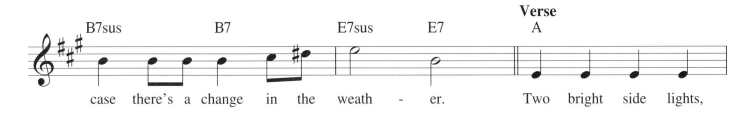

case there's a change in the weath - er. Two bright side lights,

wink - in' and blink - in'. Ain't no fin - er rig, I'm a - think - in'.

25

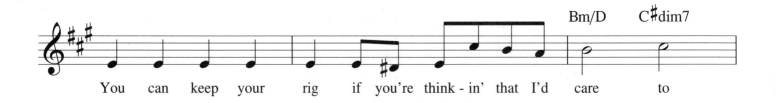
You can keep your rig if you're think-in' that I'd care to

swap for that shin-y lit-tle sur-rey with the fringe on the

Verse
In 4, sentimentally

top. I can see the stars get-tin' blur-ry,

when we ride back home in the sur-rey, rid-in' ___ slow-ly

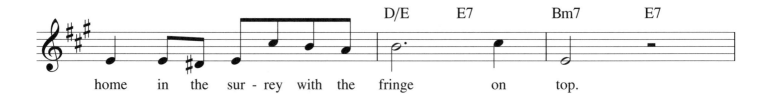
home in the sur-rey with the fringe on top.

I can feel the day get-tin' old-er, feel a sleep-y

head near my shoul-der, nod-din', droop-in'

close to my shoul-der 'til it falls, ker-plop! The

Bridge
Slightly Faster

sun is swim-min' on the rim of a hill, the

moon is tak-in' a head-er. And just as I'm think-in' all the

earth is still, a lark-'ll wake up in the med - der.

Verse - Outro
Slower, as before

Hush, you bird, my ba - by's a sleep-in'. May - be got a

dream worth a-keep-in'. Whoa, you team, and just keep a-creep-in' at a

slow clip - clop. Don't you hur - ry with the sur - rey with the

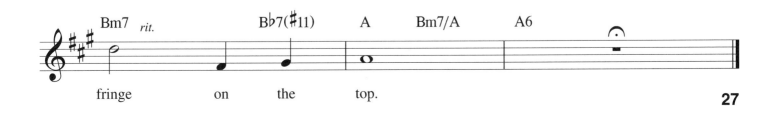

fringe on the top.

Tradition

from the Musical FIDDLER ON THE ROOF

Words by Sheldon Harnick
Music by Jerry Bock

Intro
Folk-like

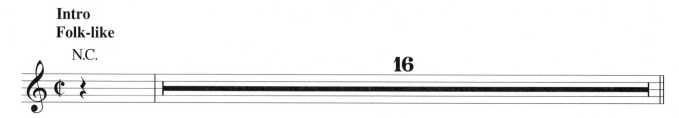

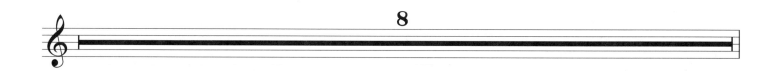

Chorus

Tra - di - tion, _____ tra - di - tion,

tra - di - tion! Tra - di - tion, _____

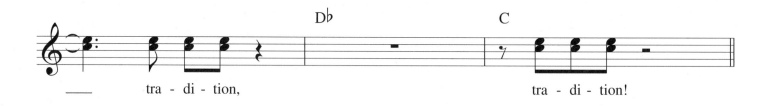

_____ tra - di - tion, tra - di - tion!

Verse

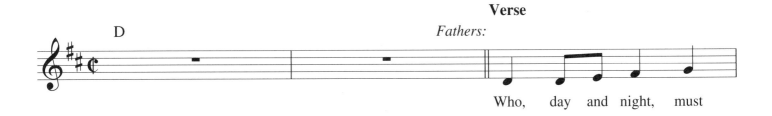

Fathers:

Who, day and night, must

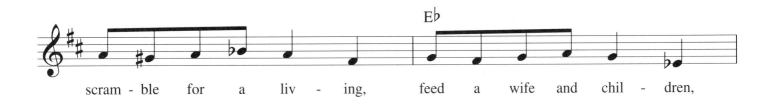

scram - ble for a liv - ing, feed a wife and chil - dren,

say his dai - ly prayers? And who has the right as

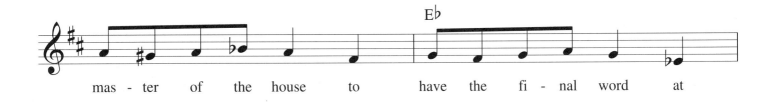

mas - ter of the house to have the fi - nal word at

Chorus

All:

home? The Pa - pa, _____ the Pa - pa.

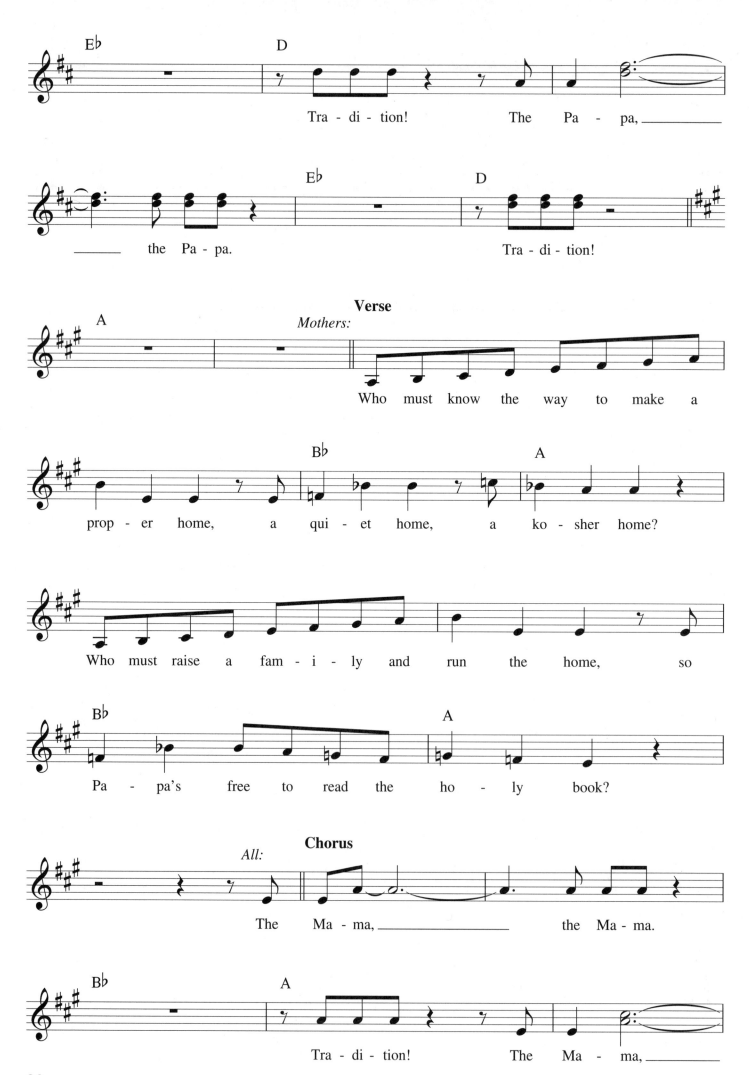

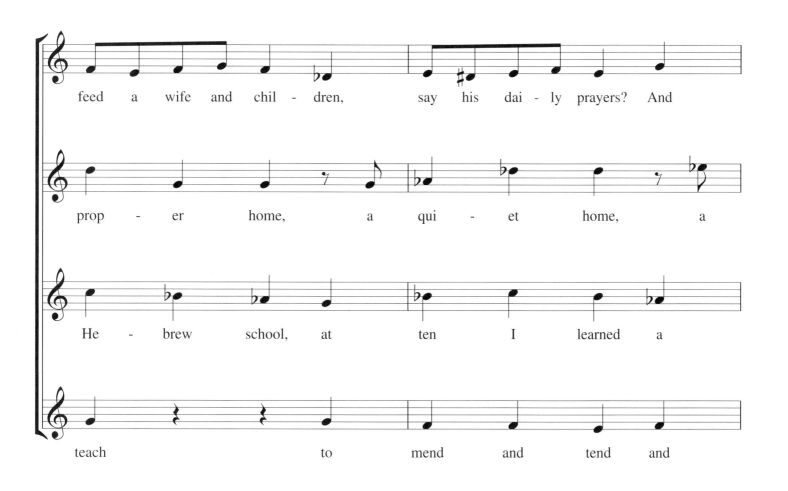

feed a wife and chil - dren, say his dai - ly prayers? And

prop - er home, a qui - et home, a

He - brew school, at ten I learned a

teach to mend and tend and

who has the right as mas - ter of the house to

ko - sher home? Who must raise a fam - i - ly and

trade. I hear they picked a

fix, pre - par - ing me to

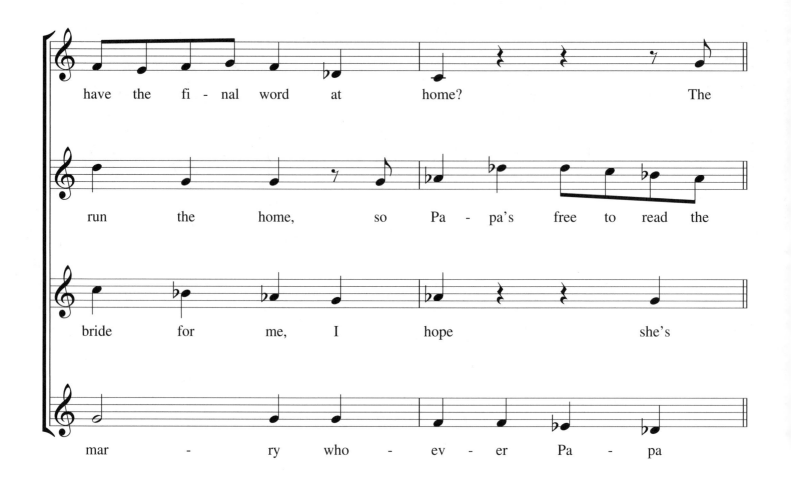

have the fi - nal word at home? The

run the home, so Pa - pa's free to read the

bride for me, I hope she's

mar - ry who - ev - er Pa - pa

Chorus

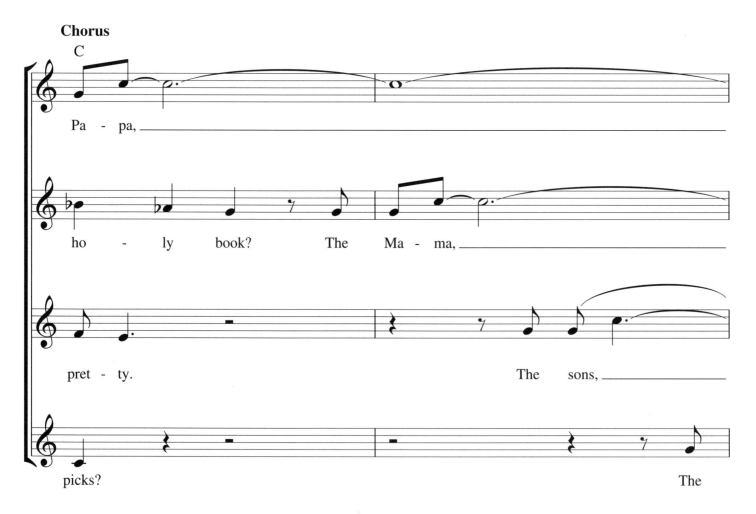

Pa - pa,

ho - ly book? The Ma - ma,

pret - ty. The sons,

picks? The

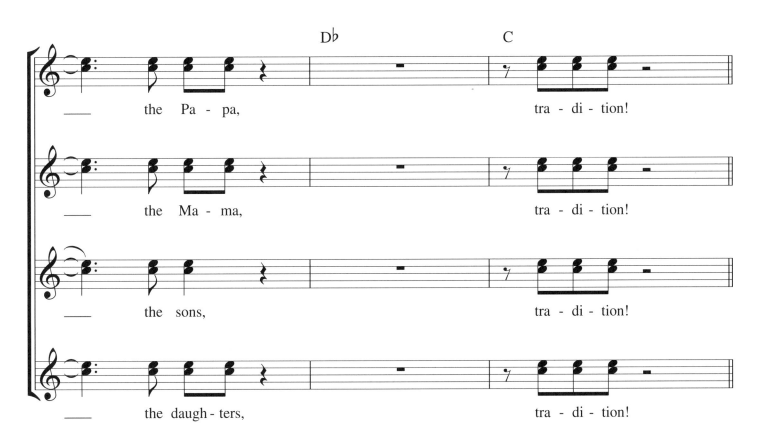

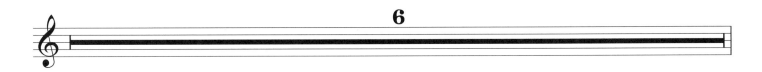

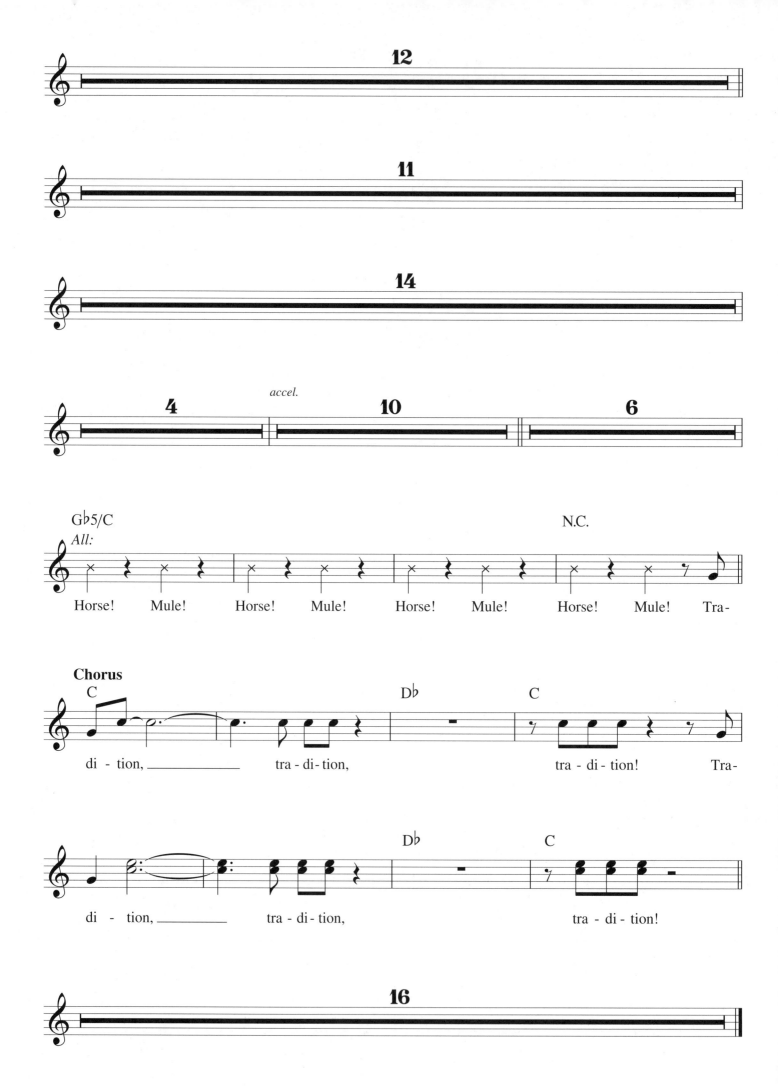

Young At Heart

from **YOUNG AT HEART**

Words by Carolyn Leigh
Music by Johnny Richards

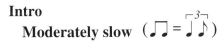

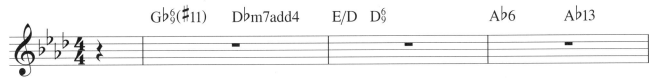

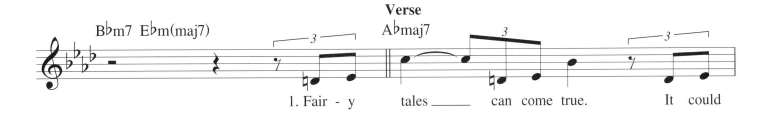

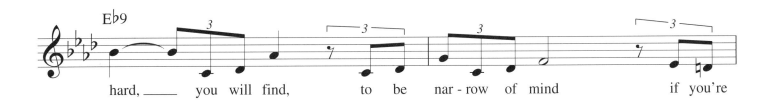

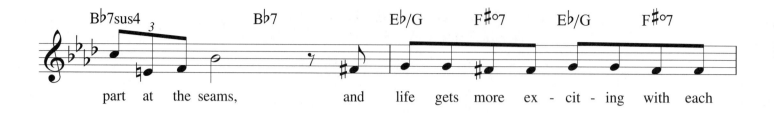

part at the seams, and life gets more ex - cit - ing with each

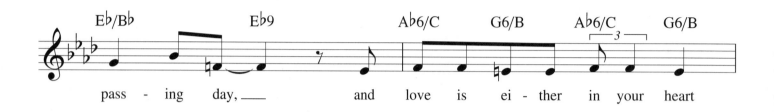

pass - ing day, ___ and love is ei - ther in your heart

Verse

or on its way. _ 2. Don't you know ___ that it's worth ev - 'ry

2nd time, Instrumental

treas-ure on earth to be young at heart? _ For as

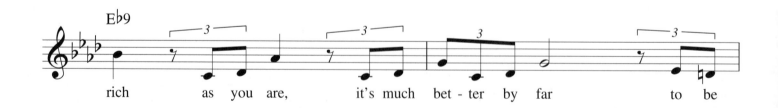

rich as you are, it's much bet - ter by far to be

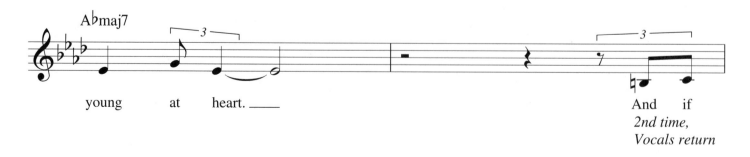

young at heart. ____ And if

2nd time,
Vocals return

you ____ should sur-vive   to   a   hun-dred and   five, ____   look at all _

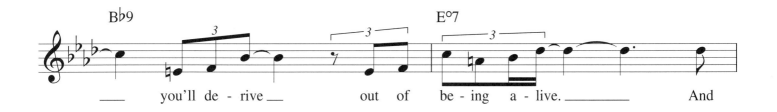

____ you'll de-rive ____   out   of   be - ing   a - live. _____   And

here   is   the   best   part, ____   you   have   a   head   start ____

To Coda

D.S. al Coda

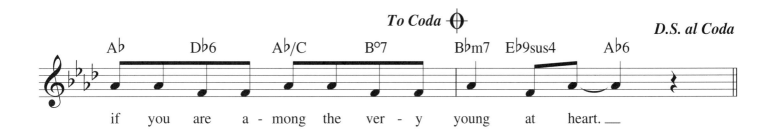

if   you   are   a - mong   the   ver - y   young   at   heart. __

Coda

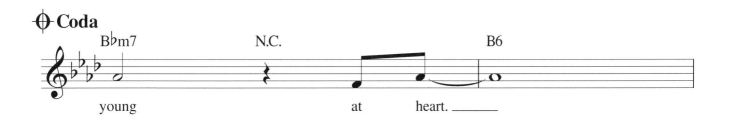

young   at   heart. _____

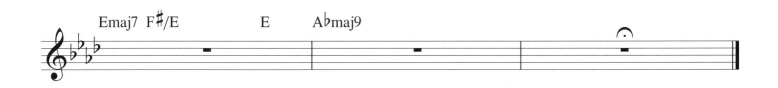